The School

Julie Murray

Abdo

Kids

MY COMMUNITY: PLACES

abdopublishing.com

Published by Abdo Kids, a division of ABDO, PO Box 398166, Minneapolis, Minnesota 55439.
Copyright © 2017 by Abdo Consulting Group, Inc. International copyrights reserved in all countries.
No part of this book may be reproduced in any form without written permission from the publisher.

Printed in the United States of America, North Mankato, Minnesota.

052016

092016

Photo Credits: iStock, Shutterstock

Production Contributors: Teddy Borth, Jennie Forsberg, Grace Hansen

Design Contributors: Christina Doffing, Candice Keimig, Dorothy Toth

Cataloging-in-Publication Data

Names: Murray, Julie, author.

Title: The school / by Julie Murray.

Description: Minneapolis, MN : Abdo Kids, [2017] | Series: My community: places
    | Includes bibliographical references and index.

Identifiers: LCCN 2015959213 | ISBN 9781680805406 (lib. bdg.) |
    ISBN 9781680805963 (ebook) | ISBN 9781680806526 (Read-to-me ebook)

Subjects: LCSH: Schools--Juvenile literature. | Buildings--Juvenile literature.

Classification: DDC 371--dc23

LC record available at http://lccn.loc.gov/2015959213

Table of Contents

The School

Jane rides the bus.

It is taking her to school.

A school is a special place.

It is where people learn.

Teachers are there.

Ms. Coy teaches math.

Students are there.

Jack reads.

Students sit in desks.

Pete does his work.

Emily is on the computer.

She types her paper.

Will is in the lunchroom.

He eats with his friends.

It is **recess**!

Mary plays outside.

What do you like about school?

At the School

computer

students

desk

teacher

Glossary

recess
a short time during the school day when students can play.

teacher
a person whose job it is to teach students about certain subjects.

Index

abdokids.com

Use this code to log on to abdokids.com and access crafts, games, videos, and more!

Abdo Kids Code:

MTK5406